TOMORROW'S SCIENCE

Internet Technologies

KU-051-558

NEWCASTLE-UNDER-LYME
COLLEGE LEARNING
RESOURCES
004 6 ROO
DC030196

Anne Rooney

Chrysalis Children's Books

Artificial Intelligence
Genetic Engineering
Internet Technologies
Medicine Now

Visit the Chrysalis website
www.chrysalisbooks.co.uk
for teachers' notes to
accompany this series.

First published in the UK in 2003 by
Chrysalis Children's Books,
64 Brewery Road, London N7 9NT

Copyright © Chrysalis Books PLC 2003

All rights reserved. No part of this book may be reproduced or utilized in any form
or by any means, electronic or mechanical, including photocopying, recording or
by any information storage and retrieval system, without permission in writing
from the publisher, except by a reviewer who may quote brief passages in a review.

Editorial manager	Joyce Bentley
Editor	Susie Brooks
Designer:	John Jamieson
Consultant:	Helen Cameron
Picture researcher:	Louise Daubeny

Also thanks to: Gill Adams, Senior Inspector, CEA@Islington; Bill Thompson; Penny Worms.

Anne Rooney asserts her moral right to be recognised as the author of this work.
If you have any comments on this book, please email her at anne@annerooney.co.uk.
For more information on her work, visit www.annerooney.co.uk.

ISBN 184138 869 6

British Library Cataloguing in Publication Data for this book is available from the British Library.

A BELITHA BOOK

Printed in Hong Kong

Picture Acknowledgements

All reasonable efforts have been made to trace the relevant copyright holders of the images contained within this
book. If we were unable to reach you, please contact Chrysalis Children's Books.
B = bottom; L = left; R = right; T = top

Front cover (foreground) Digital Vision (background) David H. Wells/Corbis 1 H&S Produktion/Corbis
4 Bettmann/Corbis 5 B David H. Wells/Corbis 6 Mug Shots/Corbis 7 www.amazon.com 8 Steve Chenn/Corbis
9 L Eric Audras/Image State 9 R Sam Ogden/SPL 10 Pisit Jiropas/Pictor/Image State 11 Bettmann/Corbis 12 Roger
Ressmeyer/Corbis 13 www.travelport.hu 14 Bubbles/Angela Hampton 15 H&S Produktion/Corbis 16 Joel
Stettenheim/Corbis 17 Ed Bock/Corbis 18 Jose Luis Pelaez, Inc./Corbis 20 Bubbles/Frans-Rombout 21 Bettmann/
Corbis 23 Karen Robinson/Rex Features 24 T Peter Turnley/Corbis 24 B Spencer Platt/Getty Images 25 Robin
Laurance/Impact Photos 26 Kevin Fleming/Corbis 27 L reproduced by kind permission of www.simputer.org
27 R David Turnley/Corbis 28 John-Marshall Mantel/Corbis 29 T Bubbles/Loisjoy Thurstun 29 B Richard Young/
Rex Features 30 Stuart Westmorland/Getty Images 32 Corbis 33 Bubbles/Frans-Rombout 34 www.spy-software-
online.com 35 Ghislain & Marie David de Lossy/Getty Images 36 Charles Sykes/Rex Features 37 reproduced
by kind permission of Tesco 38 Bubbles/Angela Hampton 39 Ariel Skelley/Corbis 40 Wolfgang Kaehler/Corbis
41 Charles & Josette Lenars/Corbis 43 Tek Image/SPL 44 Ed Kashi/Corbis.

Contents

The Internet today

You probably use the Internet quite a lot – you may even use it every day. But do you ever pause to think about how it's changing people's lives, or about the impact the Internet might have on people who don't have access to it? Computer technologies change very quickly, and often it's hard to predict how these changes will affect society.

In this book we'll look at the role the Internet plays in our lives, and think about some of the questions that are raised by its development. These are difficult but intriguing issues about what it is right and wrong to do – how we should use the Internet, and how we shouldn't. There may be no 'right' answers, but they are questions we must all think about if we are to play an active part as citizens and have a say in how our world develops.

This book won't tell you what to think. It will give you some technical background and suggest many different views and possibilities. Then you can think about and discuss the issues, forming your own opinions – opinions that you are able to explain and defend.

Computers have been around since the middle of the 20th century, but to start with they were big and slow, and very few people used them. Personal computers (PCs) became popular and developed rapidly in the 1980s and 90s.

CAMBRIDGE UNIVERSITY ONLINE CATALOGUE SYSTEM

University Library Main Building - Main Catalogue
University Library Main Building - Interim Catalogue
Union Catalogue of Departmental & College Libraries
   replaced by http://newton.lib.cam.ac.uk:7703/
4. Cambridge Union List of Serials
5. Cambridge Libraries Directory (including abbreviation

With no pictures, colours, sound, video or Flash, the original Internet was dreary to look at.

Internet or web?

Many people use the terms 'Internet' and 'world wide web' to mean the same thing. In fact, there is a difference. The Internet is the name for the worldwide network of computers that are connected and communicate with each other. The web is the set of linked pages, or websites, that we access using the Internet.

one was ever really in charge. There is still no one in charge. Some parts of the web are organised – the allocation of domain names (web addresses), for instance. But no one checks what gets put on the web and it has no internationally accepted rules. Many people think this is good; others think we need controls.

Growth of the Internet

The Internet started in the 1960s, long before the world wide web. It was first used by universities and some big businesses. They could send email, use bulletin boards and news-groups and play simple games, but all this was text-based. It wasn't until 1990, when the web was set up, that the Internet became more colourful and caught the public imagination. Along with sending email, browsing the web became the most popular online activity. Many uses have been found for the web, including games, shopping, chat and instant messaging.

Who rules the web?

The world wide web has now grown to several billion pages. This huge development wasn't planned, so no

In Singapore and some other countries, there are very strict rules about what anyone can see on the web. Yet elsewhere people can look at almost anything.

The Internet today
Changing patterns

The growth in use of the Internet has been very rapid. At the start of the 1990s few people had ever used it, but by the year 2000 about half of the households in the USA – and a third in Britain – had a computer with Internet access.

Who's online?

The change hasn't been the same worldwide. While people in the USA, Western Europe, Australasia and Southeast Asia have been doing more and more online, most people in Africa, Eastern Europe, South America, Russia and parts of Asia have still never used a computer.

Within countries, too, there are groups of people who use the Internet all the time and groups who may never use it. If you are young, reasonably wealthy and educated, you're probably quite at home on the web. If you're old, disadvantaged or live in a rural area with poor communication links, you're less likely to use it much, if at all.

Changing lives

For those of us who do use the Internet a lot, things have changed dramatically over the last decade or

Some countries have schemes that try to make computers and the Internet available to everyone. But people need training if they are new to the technology, and this is expensive.

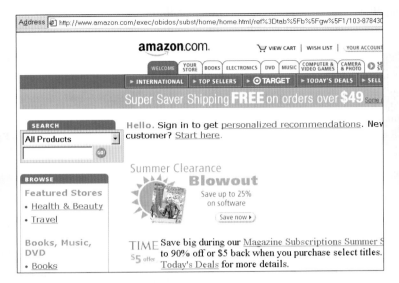

We can buy almost anything on the web, from almost anywhere in the world. The Internet is changing our shopping habits as well as other areas of our lives.

so. We can find out information, immediately, online. We can do our shopping; book tickets; manage our money; buy and sell in online auctions; communicate with distant friends and relatives quickly and cheaply; and perhaps even work from home, or while away on a trip.

It may be unfair, but some of the best deals are only available online. Someone who can afford Internet access can get, for example, cheap flights and good interest on their savings. But those without this privilege end up paying more and getting less. Can we stop these people falling behind as society moves on?

Making choices

Not everyone wants to use the Internet for everyday tasks. Some people prefer the personal service offered by a high street bank, shop or travel agent, and object to the anonymity of the web. They may feel insecure about typing their details into a computer, or unsure about the product they are purchasing. Perhaps they'd rather pay a bit more to get what they want than worry about having to search for it online.

Online crime

What's more, the Internet can hold dangers. As its popularity has grown, the web has been used increasingly to publish unpleasant material. It's also the scene of new forms of crime. Criminals can break into computers that are connected to the Internet and steal information. People send out viruses, disrupting work on other computers. Illegal information, such as how to make banned drugs or carry out terrorist attacks, is shared internationally. How can we stop criminal use of the Internet while keeping it free for everyone else to use as they wish? These are issues we'll come back to later in the book.

The Internet today
Where will it end?

These days we're not only able to do more on the Internet – we can also access it in more ways and from many more places.

Speeding up

Our connections to the Internet are now quicker than ever – and increased connection speeds make a huge difference to what we can do online. Five years ago, watching video on the Internet was almost impossible – the connection was just too slow. But now we can listen to live music and watch live video on a fast system. We can watch web TV and webcasts of concerts and other events we couldn't get to in the real world. Soon we may be able to use the web to watch films and do many more things we can't yet imagine.

New technologies

With wireless network connections and the next generation of mobile phones, we can use our computers

Tiny hand-held computers and many mobile phones can be used for email and web browsing – we can carry our web connection in our pocket.

computers that will give us online access from our jewellery or clothes! The Internet will become ever more central to our lives.

These computer glasses project a screen only the wearer can see. They can be used to access the web. Is this the look of the future?

Using a public access point, you can pick up your email or browse the web even if you don't have a computer of your own.

and browse the web wherever we go. A wireless network connection doesn't need to be plugged in – you can go online from your garden or on the train, using radio waves to carry the information.

There are web browsing booths, like public phone booths, in libraries and sports centres, hospitals and even on the streets. Cybercafés in cities around the world mean you can use your own email, and maybe even connect to your computer at home, from wherever you are. Researchers are also developing wearable

Hidden concerns

Unfortunately, while our freedom on the web increases, so do potential risks. These don't just take the form of online crime and unpleasant sites. As we use the Internet more, details about us are collected by a growing number of organisations. How these details are used and passed on worries many people – we can no longer tell who knows what about us.

No one foresaw these problems, but more could arise as developments continue. We need to think now about how we want to use and manage the Internet in the future.

What's it to you?

Why should you be concerned about the Internet? In this country Internet access is legally available to everyone, and you can go online from various different places. But the Internet holds dangers that could threaten you directly. And there are global issues that involve you, too. How the Internet affects people in other parts of the world has an impact on you, as it shapes world politics and the world economy.

Protection

Anyone can put up information on a website. There's no one checking whether it is true, accurate or good. Some people think there should be some control. But views on what should or shouldn't be allowed – what we need protecting from and who needs protecting – differ widely.

Maybe we all need protecting from pornography. Or perhaps adults should be free to see this. Maybe people shouldn't be allowed to spread information that could cause unrest or violence – but different people have different views on what information this would be.

A website is kept, or 'hosted', on a computer that can be anywhere in the world. Some countries have laws about what may and may not be shown on the web. Sites hosted in these places can be taken down if they're illegal. But some countries have no rules of this kind.

Many remote places have no laws regarding the Internet. One of these places could be used to host a website that's illegal elsewhere.

Freedom

In some countries, people are allowed to say what they think, however much it may hurt or upset others. This is called freedom of speech. Freedom of information is also highly valued in many places. The law gives people a right to know what's going on, even if making the knowledge available may have damaging results. In other countries, information is held back – but keeping people in the dark can also be damaging.

Should we be allowed to say things that will damage others? Is our right to do what we want greater than someone else's right to be unharmed? How can we balance people's rights as individuals with what we need to know to keep society secure? All these issues come to the fore with the Internet. How can we make sure it is used for everyone's benefit?

Freedom of speech can lead to better understanding between people. But freedom of speech on the Internet can also help people to spread racial prejudice or abuse specific groups of people.

Over to you

We all have a right to be involved in decisions about the world's future. But in order to have the power to change things, we need to understand the issues that affect us all. You will need to be able to separate fact from opinion in the things you read and hear. You will need to be able to disentangle reliable information from media scare stories and public relations hype. If you can do this, and shape your own informed views, you will be able to play an important part in the changing world. Use the 'Ask yourself' boxes in the following chapters as a starting point for discussing the issues raised.

Keeping information safe

Businesses will pay a lot of money to get hold of someone's personal information, if they think they can make a profit from it. They might, for example, want a person's contact details in order to try to sell them something. The Internet makes it very easy for people to share – and steal – information of this kind. How could it affect you?

Information today can be shared globally at the click of a button. Can we control what happens to information about ourselves?

The law on your side

Many countries have laws that protect people from information about them being misused. In the UK, for example, the Data Protection Act states that people who want to store information about others must first register with the Information Commissioner. They have to say what they are going to do with the information, agree to use it only for the purpose specified, and let any person see a copy of the information held on them.

This means that your school is allowed to hold information about you that's useful to them in educating

There are rules for use of personal information in the UK. But do you know what Hungarian law allows people to do with your details if you submit them on the web?

you and looking after you. But they're not allowed to sell your details to a company that might want to encourage you to join a film club, for example.

National boundaries

Laws about what can be done with personal details vary from country to country. An organisation in the UK will have to follow UK rules. But if information about you is kept on a computer in another country, British law may not protect you. Someone will have to tell you if they move your details to, say, the USA – but once they are there, US law applies. If you type your details into a web page hosted in Poland, Polish law applies.

The European Union (EU) and the USA are currently arguing about what can be done with information about people. At the moment, they allow different things. Where does that leave you? You probably don't know what information is held about you, or where, or what people are allowed to do with it.

Case study

Recently, a UK-based online computer store moved its customer records to the USA. Customers were asked to agree to their records being transferred abroad, where they would be subject to US law rather than UK law. But how many people would know what the move might mean to them – whether in the USA their details might be sold to people who send out junk mail, for instance?

Ask yourself

◆ Is it fair that your personal details can be sold and stored all around the world?
◆ Do you have a right to know who has information on you, and where it's kept?
◆ Do you have a right to look at the information and change it or have it removed if you wish?
◆ How could this be managed globally?

Keeping information safe

Hackers and criminals

People who break into computer systems by dodging passwords, or by other means, are called hackers. Many hackers break into systems for fun – just to prove they can. They might leave something like a coded message or picture to show they've been there, but not do any real harm.

Other hackers break in to disrupt a system or to steal information. Many people fear that hackers will break into their bank account, or take their credit card details from a computer and use them to shop. People may also worry that someone could access secret information and use it to blackmail them. Or a hacker might be hired for a revenge attack – harming someone by sending abusive email in their name, for instance. Private detectives no longer just follow people and listen in to their phone calls. Now they can pay a hacker to find out all about someone by accessing their computer files and maybe intercepting their email.

No secrets

A hacker can often find out all someone's personal details – about their money, their education, their work history, their family, and their medical health. Organisations are

Trade in stolen information is growing. Some hackers will find out anything you want to know about a person for less than £100.

Case study

An ex-employee of Elite Web Hosting in Florida, USA, was so annoyed with the company that he carried out a revenge attack. He hacked into their computer system and sent out abusive emails to customers, suggesting that the company was moving into pornography. Elite went bankrupt as a result, but did not prosecute the culprit because they felt the damage had already been done and that legal action would be a waste of money.

The Internet is not always secure. Someone who sets up one-click buying on a computer in a library or cybercafé may find themselves paying for everyone else's shopping.

required by law to keep this information safe. But good hackers can break into almost any computer system, including those in large corporations and governments. Even without hackers, all computer systems are vulnerable because they are operated by people – and people can make mistakes, act wrongly, misunderstand what they are meant to do, or accept money to reveal secrets. Once information is on a computer system, it could be at risk.

Safe shopping?

Some shopping and other websites encourage users to set up 'one-click buying'. For people who use the same computer and credit card all the time, this is a quick way of shopping. Instead of giving their credit card details every time they want to buy something, the details are stored on computer. The sites urge people to use this only in a safe place – such as at home – but even then it's risky. If anyone sees your one-click account details, they can use your money.

Ask yourself

◆ Is it the responsibility of the organisation that puts up a website, or of the individual user, to make sure that personal details are kept safe?
◆ If someone lost money because they didn't understand the risk of setting up one-click buying on a library computer, is that their own fault? Or should the website – or the library – not allow them to do it?

Censoring the web

You can find almost anything on the web if you know where to look. Is this a good thing, or should there be some restrictions on what's available?

Some of the material on the Internet is far more unpleasant than anything that is allowed in films, books, magazines or on TV. Most countries have laws about what can be published in print or shown on screen. Should the web be any different?

Censorship

Censorship is the restriction of what people are allowed to see, hear or read. It can be used to protect people from material that could damage or upset them. And it can be used to restrict people's freedom, by controlling their access to information that they might use in undesirable ways.

There is no worldwide censorship of the web, but most countries have laws that apply to the web as well as to other media. In the UK, for example, certain types of pornography are illegal. The material can't be sold in print, shown in films or published on a UK website. But there is nothing stopping us viewing pornography that's been published on a website elsewhere. As the Internet is international, anyone in the UK can look at a site hosted abroad.

The law stops children from buying or renting videos, or seeing films, that are rated unsuitable for their age group. But children may be exposed to undesirable material, unrestricted, on the web.

What should we censor?

Different countries want different things from censoring the web. In the West, our aims tend to be to protect children and other impressionable people; to restrict pornographic or violent material; to block information that encourages crime; and to prevent people saying abusive things about other individuals or groups.

This is not the same worldwide, however. In some countries, the state might want to censor sites that suggest a way of life they don't agree with. We'll discuss this further in later chapters of the book.

Against censorship

Some people think that although it's right to protect children through censorship, adults should be free to see what they like. They say that adults should be able to choose to act responsibly and that we can't protect them from everything. For example, we expect most people to drive cars safely, even though they could kill someone with their car. People who are against censorship believe in freedom of information – they feel that there should be no limits to what people can say, see or hear in the media, on the Internet, or by other means of communication.

For censorship

Other people think that we should all be protected from the most unpleasant material. They believe that if we see too much violence, we may become hardened to it and accept or carry out violence in the real world more readily. They also argue that graphic sex or violence in films, websites or computer games can be so upsetting that it causes us emotional or psychological damage. So they believe we should ban it in the same way as we ban dangerous drugs that cause physical harm.

Some countries have strict rules banning things we may consider acceptable, such as advertising swimwear on the web.

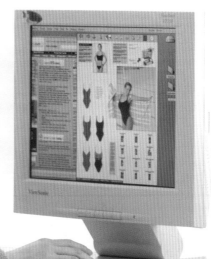

Censoring the web

Harming each other

Some sites should perhaps be censored on the basis that they give people details on how to hurt one another – sites that explain how to make weapons, or kill or torture people, for example. Information like this is available in some books, but these are difficult to get hold of. The web makes such information available to everyone.

Some websites may be intended to cause harm to particular individuals. Information such as the release dates of prisoners, along with their criminal records, can be put on a website for anyone to see. This may be to warn people that they could be in danger when the criminals are free – or it could be intended to help a victim, or relative of a victim, take revenge.

Case study

In April 1999, teenagers Dylan Klebold and Eric Harris killed 15 fellow pupils and teachers in an attack on Columbine High School, Colorado, USA. They apparently used instructions for making pipe bombs, which they had found on the Internet. Harris used a website and email to make death threats before the attack. Later the same year, another student received a death threat in an instant message and Columbine school was closed for two days.

With a little effort, anyone could find out on the web how to make a bomb like this, or an illegal drug.

Setting a bad example

Even sites that don't appear to intend harm to others can be damaging if they're seen by impressionable people. Some sites might set an example that seems unacceptable to the rest of society – promoting the positive effects of drugs, for instance. Some people might think these sites should be censored. But others would feel this violates their personal freedom.

Pro-anorexia websites promote the deadly eating disorder anorexia nervosa as a lifestyle choice. These sites could endanger vulnerable young people. For a while, international concern was enough to close most of these sites down. But as interest has shifted elsewhere, the sites have returned.

Ask yourself

◆ Who is responsible for protecting vulnerable people in society? Is it the job of the government, the computer industry, or of individuals?
◆ Who should decide which things people should be protected from and which things are harmless?

Censoring the web

Partial protection

Rating systems are now being developed to help people restrict which websites they can see on their own computers. Some – but not all – publishers of websites rate their sites' contents, stating whether or not they include, for instance, sexual material or disturbing pictures. Parents can protect their children by installing filtering programs. Some filters work by allowing only suitably rated pages to be displayed – but as many sites aren't rated, this can be overly restrictive. Other filters try to judge what's in a page and decide whether it can or can't be seen – but they are not always reliable because they may not pick up all unpleasant material.

A lot of people use the Internet in public places such as libraries and schools. In schools, filters are generally used. But this isn't always the case with cybercafés and libraries. In the UK and some other countries, some kind of filtering is usually in place, but in the USA unlimited access is generally allowed.

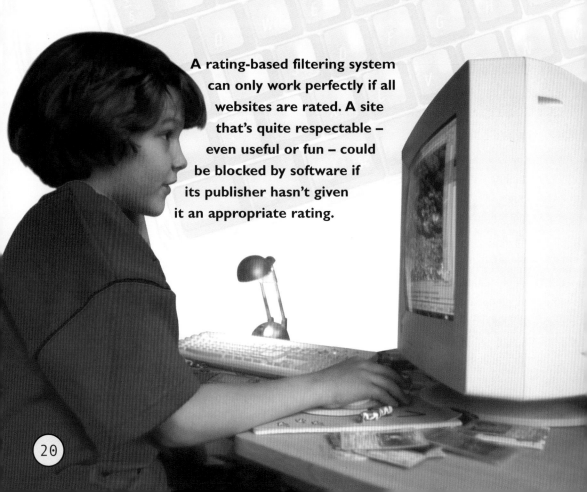

A rating-based filtering system can only work perfectly if all websites are rated. A site that's quite respectable – even useful or fun – could be blocked by software if its publisher hasn't given it an appropriate rating.

> *'We know that there are children out there whose parents do not take the kind of interest in their upbringing and in their existence that we would wish, but I don't think censorship is ever the solution to any problem.'*
>
> Judith Krug, American Library Association

Ask yourself

◆ If public money is used to supply Internet access points in libraries and other buildings, should these enable people to see whatever they like? Or should they block access to pornography and other content that many people object to?

In some areas of the world there is a no man's land between states or countries, where no laws exist. Could cyberspace be the new no man's land, with no rules and no international agreement?

Whose choice?

If we decided that the content of web pages should be controlled, we would need to appoint a body of people to check all web pages and rate each one. We have a system like this for rating films, but it doesn't apply internationally. A film distributor has to be granted certification in each different country that will show the film. To apply this system to the Internet would be a phenomenal – perhaps impossible – task. There are, of course, many more websites created each year than films.

At the moment, the USA is trying to become the country that polices the web. Many people object to this as they don't share America's views. Maybe in the future we'll see a regional splitting of the web, with one section of the Internet overseen by the USA, and another – or many others – overseen by countries with different value systems.

Ask yourself

◆ Who would be trusted to check and rate websites?
◆ How would we pick the conditions by which a website should be allowed?
◆ Could ratings be international?
◆ How would cultural differences between countries be treated?

Limited access

There are some countries in which Internet use is restricted by the government. People either aren't allowed the equipment to access the Internet, or they can only look at a restricted set of sites. Does a country have the right to impose these rules?

'Everyone shall have the right...
to receive and impart information
and ideas of all kinds, regardless
of frontiers.'

UNITED NATIONS' INTERNATIONAL COVENANT ON CIVIL AND POLITICAL RIGHTS, ARTICLE 19 (1966)

Internet bans

You might not be allowed to go online sometimes because it's too expensive or ties up the phone line – but it's not illegal. In Myanmar (previously Burma) it's illegal to own a modem, send email or use the web unless you have permission. Owning a modem without permission can land you in jail for up to 15 years.

Myanmar isn't the only country with restrictions. In Iraq, Libya and North Korea, Internet access is completely banned. Elsewhere, governments block sites of which they don't approve.

Countries with major Internet restrictions, 1999

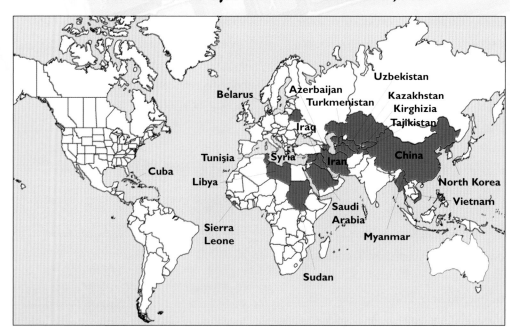

Why ban access?

The Internet is dominated by the West and particularly by the USA. Many countries don't share Western views. There may be religious, cultural and political reasons for wanting to keep Western websites from people.

Some of the material available on the web is also against the law in many places. For instance, a website on brewing beer will be illegal in countries where alcohol isn't allowed.

Politics

Many countries try to stop people forming groups or sharing information that might lead them to rebel against their government. This includes information published on the Internet. Through the Internet, people in these countries may learn about political systems that would otherwise be unknown to them. This might inspire them to challenge their own systems.

Countries such as Iran ban or limit Internet access because they fear their way of life will change if people are influenced by Western ideas.

They may be helped by people outside their country via email or online chat.

How you view this will depend on who you are and what you believe. We might think it wrong to publish information that could damage a government. But in a country ruled by a dictator who imprisons and tortures people, the Internet might be the lifeline the people need – and for that very reason be banned.

Ask yourself

◆ Does a country have a right to try to preserve its own way of life by blocking websites that promote different views?
◆ How can we decide whether we are being restricted or protected?

Limited access

In 1989 Chinese students rioted and campaigned for new rights and an end to their Communist government. If wanting a Western lifestyle leads to civil unrest, is a country right to block access to Western ideas on the Internet?

Human rights

In some countries, access to Western news sites or the sites of human rights organisations is banned. The Chinese, for example, argue that they disagree with the way US news sites interpret the news. After the terrorist attacks on the USA in September 2001, the Chinese people wanted more detailed information. The government eased restrictions on the web, but continued to block many major US news sites. They have also maintained a ban on

human rights sites – such as www.amnesty.org – which they feel will encourage their people to question the way they are treated.

Ask yourself

◆ Can a country justify banning access to human rights sites on the Internet?
◆ Should a government control what its people see and read, or should the people be trusted to make up their own minds?

Human rights organisations, such as Amnesty International, fight for people to be well treated throughout the world, regardless of cultural, political or religious background.

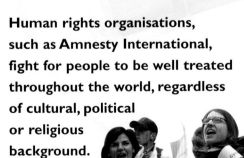

Religious rights

Much of our lifestyle is bound up with religious ideas – and they're not shared by everyone in the world. Some of the images and practices that are part of everyday life in the West may be offensive to people with different traditions and beliefs. Some countries want to block Western sites and other Internet services to protect their people from material that they consider spiritually damaging.

Most religions in India discourage girls from interacting with boys. But many girls are using Internet chat services to chat with young men. Which is more important – the girls' desire for freedom or India's traditional culture?

Case study

A Council of Ministers Resolution in 2001 banned people in Saudi Arabia from looking at or publishing some types of information on the Internet. The network that connects the country to the Internet, run by the Internet Services Unit, operates a full filtering system. This blocks web pages that people aren't allowed to see, including some pages with religious or political content, and sites that show pornography or 'images of people wearing less clothes than is typical in Saudi Arabia'. This means that some sites about swimming are blocked as they show people in few clothes. Also banned are sites that promote Western music and films, sites that cover 'unsuitable' activities for women, and sites about human rights in Saudi Arabia.

Ask yourself

◆ Is banning all or most Internet access the same thing as blocking odd sites that show too much violence or provide illegal information?

◆ Is a Muslim country banning sites about alcohol any different from the UK banning sites about drugs that are illegal here?

Losing equality?

The Internet makes information available to people in a way that has never before been possible. But at the same time, those who don't have online access may become more and more cut off. Should we be protecting people from getting left behind?

Social impact

Internet use has increased hugely over the last five years or so, and about half of all people in developed Western countries use it frequently now. But are those who don't use it becoming increasingly disadvantaged?

People who are online have access to information that can help them have a better life. They can get better deals on anything from flights to bank savings and books; they can save time with online bookings and timetables; they can communicate for free, or very cheaply; and they can order their shopping from their home instead of driving to the shops.

Increased use of the web may have other consequences for society. Already banks are closing in rural areas as telephone and online banking take off. There may not be enough business for small bookshops or music stores to survive as more people buy products online. Losing banks and shops will have most impact on older people and those who can't afford cars – the very people who are less likely to use the Internet.

Cybercafés and libraries worldwide have made the Internet available to many more people – but some are still too wary, or just not interested. Should we allow these people to be at a disadvantage?

The simputer is a cheap, hand-held device that can be used for Internet access. Users don't need to be able to read or write. Devices such as this can be used in remote villages around the world. They are often given by charities. Could they help developing countries to catch up?

Politics online

In many countries, government information is now available online. People who use the Internet will have the chance to find out more about political and social issues that affect them. But people who aren't online will have less information. They may not find out about future plans that could affect them, or about benefits (money) they are entitled to claim.

Some areas are planning to introduce online voting for elections. This would mean that people could vote from home. At the moment, one of the things that stops people voting is the need to travel to a polling station. Online voting might mean

that people with Internet access would be more likely to vote than those without it, changing the balance of votes cast.

Voting usually takes place in a polling station. Will the chance to vote online change the balance of power in favour of the young, wealthy and educated who have access to the Internet at home?

Ask yourself

◆ Are we creating a world in which people will have to use the web, whether they want to or not, if they are to play a full part in social and political life?
◆ Is it fair to do this?
◆ Should special measures be taken for people who don't have, or perhaps don't want, access to a computer?

Playing fair

Not all information is intended for sharing freely. People who make a living from writing, making music or films and other creative activities can't afford to give away for free the materials they produce. But the Internet makes it easy for anyone to share – and steal – music, video and games.

E-pirates

The Internet provides a quick way of moving information to anywhere in the world – and anyone can make information available on the web. So it has become easy for people to distribute pirate (illegal) copies of videos and music online. If you know where to look, you can find current music and just-released videos to download for free. These are illegal, unauthorised versions. They may be made from stolen tapes of new films, or recorded from a real CD. If someone makes an illegal copy instead of buying one, the creators of the original don't get the money they ought to from their work.

Intellectual property

Intellectual property rights are the ownership rights that an author, composer or artist has in his or her work. They mean that you shouldn't photocopy someone's book or record their music from the radio or the web – you should pay for a real copy from which they earn their money.

Businesses have intellectual property rights to new inventions, documents they publish, ideas, films and other kinds of production. The laws covering intellectual property are intended to protect people whose work is not in making physical objects, but in creative thought.

A few authors, such as Stephen King, have embraced the influence of the web and now publish some books online.

Cheap writable CDs have made it very easy for people to copy music from CDs and from the Internet.

Ask yourself

◆ Is taking a pirate copy of a video or CD from the web any different from stealing a CD or DVD from a shop?

◆ People who can't afford a CD or DVD would probably not buy it in the first place, so there would be no loss of sale if these people downloaded pirate copies. Would this make it acceptable?

◆ Would you download a film or piece of music, knowing that it was illegal?

Case study

Napster.com was a website that ran a club for sharing music. A member of Napster could upload music from a CD they'd bought, and another Napster member could listen to it without buying a copy of the CD. This was in theory legal, as it was similar to inviting friends to your house to listen to a new CD. The problem was that the club was open to anyone, so effectively the whole world could share music without buying it. The music industry objected to this and took Napster to court. They claimed that Napster were making music available illegally. Although Napster may have had a strong case in defence, they ran out of money fighting the court action and closed down.

The music industry relies on CD sales to make money to pay for future recordings. If everyone stole pirate copies, bands would go out of business and stop making music. But CDs are expensive and the music industry makes huge profits. Does this encourage piracy?

Playing fair

Many films circulate on the Internet before they come out on DVD and video. If you could make a copy for free, would you still buy the film when it was released?

Counter measures

The video and music industries are very concerned about the number of pirate copies circulating on the web – and the pirate copies people make with the CD and DVD writers in their computers. Some CD manufacturers have tried making disks that can't be played in the CD-ROM drive of a computer – so they can't be uploaded onto a website or copied onto another CD. Some protected CDs have even corrupted the operating system of Apple computers.

Downloading software

It's easy to download software from the Internet. It falls into three groups:
◆ free software that you can use without payment
◆ commercial software that you pay for and then download
◆ shareware, which you try out for a free period and then pay for.

Shareware

You download shareware for free, but before doing so you have to agree either to pay for it after the trial period or to delete it from your computer. This often depends on trust, as you may be able to carry on using the software even if you don't pay. But if people don't pay, there won't be any money for developing more software.

Ask yourself

◆ Should people who buy a CD be allowed to play it in their computer if they want to, or copy it for private use?
◆ Is it fair to stop everyone doing this, just because a few will break the law?

Act thoughtfully

You probably use the Internet a lot to help with your homework. Sometimes, you may have copied text or pictures to use in your own work. It's easy to think that material on the web is freely available – but in fact it's all covered by copyright law. By copying a picture from a website to use in your own site, you could be breaking the law.

Fair use

Copyright law in many countries allows a small portion of a piece of copyright material to be copied

How often do you copy text or pictures from the web?

without permission as long as it counts as 'fair use'. This is not clearly defined, but includes use for education, research, to illustrate a point, and so on. Only small parts of a copyright work can be copied, and they shouldn't be used to make money. The source of the material should be shown clearly.

Ask yourself

◆ If someone stole and used an idea or story of yours from the web, how would you feel?
◆ What use do you think you should be allowed to make of material you find on the web? See if you can come up with some guidelines for fair use.

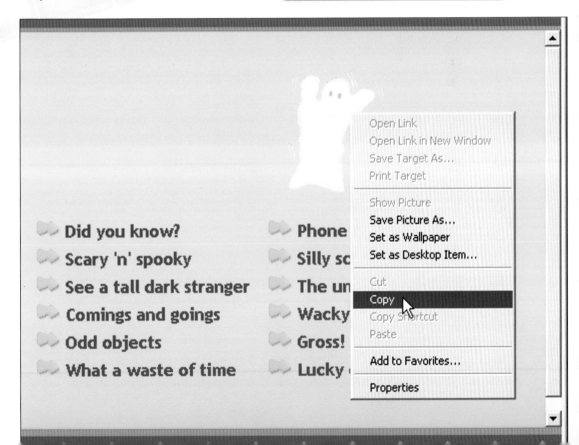

Big brother

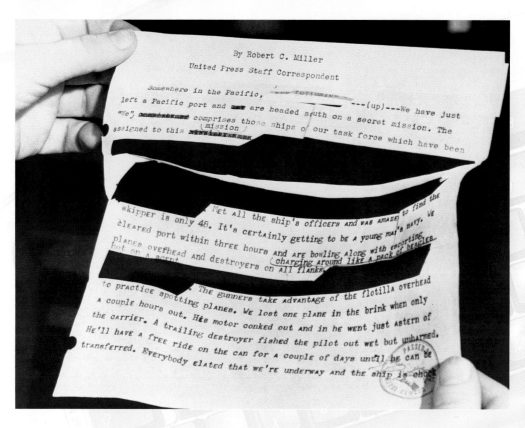

By Robert C. Miller
United Press Staff Correspondent

Somewhere in the Pacific, --- (up)---We have just left a Pacific port and *** are headed south on a secret mission. The "We", ********** comprises those ships of our task force which have been assigned to this ****** (mission)

skipper is only 48. It's certainly getting to be a young man's navy. We cleared port within three hours and are bowling along with escorting planes overhead and destroyers on all flanks, charging around like a pack of beagles hot on a scent.

The gunners take advantage of the flotilla overhead to practice spotting planes. We lost one plane in the brink when only a couple hours out. His motor conked out and in he went just astern of the carrier. A trailing destroyer fished the pilot out wet but unharmed. He'll have a free ride on the can for a couple of days until he can be transferred. Everybody elated that we're underway and the ship is chock

The Internet has made communicating and sharing information very easy – but it's also made it simple for others to tap into our communications, to see what we've been doing online and to uncover private details about us. You might be surprised at how much snooping goes on.

Always watching

There's no organisation officially checking the whole of the Internet. But if you use email, the world wide web and chat rooms, what you do on

Governments have always censored communications to keep information hidden from enemies. In World War I, the army read soldiers' letters and obscured any bits that would betray secrets if they fell into enemy hands.

your computer can be watched. Those watching could be anyone from your parents or teachers to the government of your country or of another country. These people claim they are watching for our protection – but it means we have little privacy.

Spying at work

Computer networks in schools and businesses are set up so that everyone has a personal identity – a login name and password – that lets them use their own files and email account. These are set up and looked after by a systems administrator – someone who understands the computer network and runs it.

In order to do his or her job properly, the systems administrator needs to be able to look at your work on the computer and reset your passwords. He or she can look at Internet traffic – files that are going out and coming in – including the web pages people are browsing.

The systems administrator should be trustworthy and not breach the privacy of computer users. But in many organisations, especially those that don't let people send personal emails or use the web from work, the systems administrator may be asked to check on people's computer use.

Ask yourself

◆ Is it acceptable to keep track of people's computer use at work? People are supposed to be working, so if they are taking advantage of the Internet for personal use, does the organisation have the right to check up on them?
◆ If an organisation found out something serious about an employee from tracking their email and Internet use, should they tell the police?

Someone can always tell what web pages you've been looking at and who you've been emailing.

Big brother

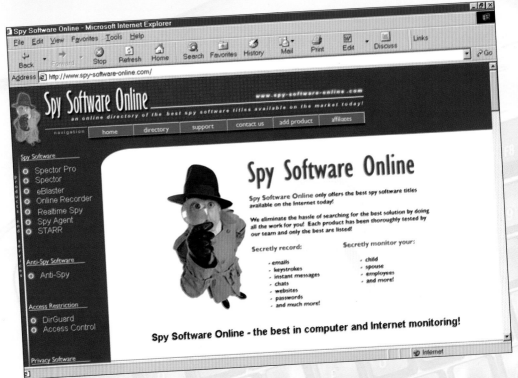

Spy Software Online - Microsoft Internet Explorer

File Edit View Favorites Tools Help

Back Forward Stop Refresh Home Search Favorites History Mail Print Edit Discuss Links

Address http://www.spy-software-online.com/

Spy Software Online
www.spy-software-online.com
an online directory of the best spy software titles available on the market today!

navigation home directory support contact us add product affiliates

Spy Software
○ Spector Pro
○ Spector
○ eBlaster
○ Online Recorder
○ Realtime Spy
○ Spy Agent
○ STARR

Anti-Spy Software
○ Anti-Spy

Access Restriction
○ DirGuard
○ Access Control

Privacy Software

Spy Software Online

Spy Software Online only offers the best spy software titles available on the Internet today!

We eliminate the hassle of searching for the best solution by doing all the work for you! Each product has been thoroughly tested by our team and only the best are listed!

Secretly record:
- emails
- keystrokes
- instant messages
- chats
- websites
- passwords
- and much more!

Secretly monitor your:
- child
- spouse
- employees
- and more!

Spy Software Online - the best in computer and Internet monitoring!

Internet

At home

It's not just computer use in organisations that's monitored – your parents may be tracking what you do on your computer at home. If your computer isn't password-protected, they might be looking at files on your hard disk and at your email. They can also look in the History folder of your web browser to see which web pages you've visited.

If they are really serious about finding out what you're doing, they can install software on your computer that tracks everything you do. You won't know it's there. Parents do this because they are worried about their

Software for spying on Internet usage is widely advertised and used, especially in the USA.

children looking at unsuitable material or chatting online with people who may do them harm.

Ask yourself

◆ Do you have a right to privacy on your computer at home?
◆ If your parents are concerned about you coming to harm, does that give them the right to see what you've been doing online and to read your email?
◆ If a parent had a serious concern – that their child was involved with drugs, for instance – would that give them the right to spy in this way?

Echelon

Every email you write, every phone call you make and every text message you send on your mobile could be scanned by software for Echelon. Echelon is a large, international surveillance system that tries to track all the satellite communications around the world. Millions of calls and messages are intercepted every day, and software is used to scan each one. It's estimated that about one in every thousand communications is picked up by the scans as suspicious. In these cases, the messages go to a person for checking. Only one in a thousand of these suspicious messages is ever passed on to the security services for further investigation.

Some people are more likely to be targets of Echelon than others. Politicians, trade union leaders, important figures in businesses or human rights organisations, and even church leaders, will be more closely watched than other people.

Civil liberties

Many people are concerned about communications being intercepted by systems like Echelon. They argue that it invades privacy and means that our civil liberties – our rights as citizens – are being ignored.

Ask yourself

◆ If you're not committing any criminal offences, is it acceptable that the state (or anyone else) can intercept your communications?
◆ Do we have a right to keep secrets?

Would you be more careful about what you said on the phone if you knew someone was checking up on your conversations?

Big brother

Secrets and security

The authorities argue that they need to be able to track and read communications to help in the fight against crime. Yet a person may want to keep something secret even if it's not illegal. They may be homosexual and think that other people knowing would affect their job, for example. Secrets don't remain truly secret if they are mentioned at all online.

New York's Twin Towers were destroyed by terrorists on September 11, 2001. Security agencies want to intercept communications to fight this type of crime. Is it fair that they can do so at the expense of our privacy?

```
-----BEGIN PGP MESSAGE-----
Version: PGPfreeware 7.0.3 for non-c

qANQR1DBwU4DX+RePHhsPosQB/9d53xrmZnR
Zt+sa9hKuEHDp7oJ5W/BzOT+FezdobgKM2Ux
DgkE9GsjUkg9ydWxr3qRaPt76cLNLvuFczUb
s5W9r5olhTy7dt+7BfttOCRVo+7iRwjofUQH
+CR+AknlghnY7oNhNee5Q2emQHd77u/AegYz
GiVZV+Ux5n/LXYqUyUW21r86dq+X5ItczROU
8380VfJJdvIrHmxo9cCXRCBZ8ffhfdOapuVR
irpDBBSQOjQh+2kgaSeFVe6O/bu15j71WKAy
GsOW4Pk/iD6WhL3sOO+rL/RD6FSq7sikKEGu
BRQ4JT1mV2LBGfI1HiB3Da8MdQzdMwsf2qhw
b9Z9Gpbgdt+iexeRkNKyqNlDE77zdwFFVtCB
```

An encrypted document like this can only be opened using a coded 'key'. It won't make sense to anyone who doesn't know the key.

Encryption

Encryption means using a secret code to keep a communication private. Computer documents and emails can be encrypted using very powerful codes that are extremely hard to break, even using other computers.

It is illegal to export the most powerful encryption technologies from the USA. The US government doesn't want other countries to use communication methods that it can't break into. In some countries, encryption itself is illegal. In the UK, if you have a file encrypted on your hard disk and are investigated, you have to open it. If you forget the password and can't open it, you can be imprisoned.

Trapdoors and software

It's not just the government and people around you who are watching you. Some pieces of software have a 'trapdoor' that means someone else can get access to the program, or to your whole computer. In this way, information can be stolen without you knowing it. The information can be what software you've got or which web pages you've visited, or even the content of files on your hard disk.

If you install the program RealPlayer on your computer to play music and other audio files, you will find that it often tries to access the Internet, even when you don't need it to. When you play music, it sends a copy of your playlist (the tracks you're playing) to a database collecting information about what music people are listening to. This might sound quite harmless – but programs of this type can gather other information from your system to send out, too. If your computer is online all the time – which many now are – information can be sent out without you knowing about it at all.

Case study

Loyalty cards are used by stores to gather information about what people buy. When the card is swiped, a record of items bought is stored on a computer database. The shop uses this to help with their marketing by sending customers specially targeted offers. Recently, the UK government asked for the information from supermarkets' databases so that it could compare people's shopping habits with health records. They argued that this would help them to make links between diet and health and enable them to plan healthcare for the future. Supermarkets refused to hand over the information in this instance, but new regulations could mean the government would be able to force the supermarkets to part with customers' details.

A loyalty card collects information about you. Should governments have a right to this information?

Ask yourself

◆ Should computer programs be able to send out information in this way?
◆ Should you need to give permission for a program to send information from your computer?

That's rubbish!

You've probably been told at some point to stop playing online games and to do something more valuable with your time. But how much does it matter if we spend a lot of time online?

A waste of time?

Research into frequent computer use has come up with varied results. Some studies have found that, because using the Internet is a solitary activity, it can damage social skills. People who spend long periods of time alone may find it hard to relate to others. They might find conversation difficult, or feel shy in public. In this way, the isolation a computer provides could be damaging to society.

The web may also draw people away from other activities, such as sport or reading books, which some people would argue are more beneficial.

But other studies suggest that regular computer use can be a positive thing. People who shy away from social situations in favour of online games and so on, will often become very good at programming and other computer technologies. Likewise, many games can improve skills such as reflexes, logic and visual awareness.

Using a computer is a solitary activity that doesn't help us develop social skills. But does it have benefits?

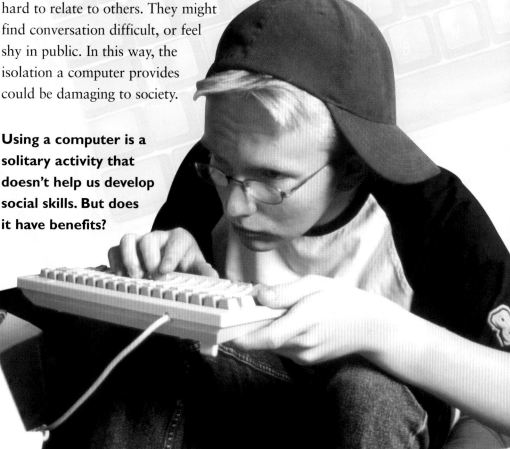

Should we spend our free time profitably, like these community volunteers, or is it up to us what we do with our leisure time?

Quality and content

Some material on the web is of a very high quality. It can be educational, cultural, useful and enjoyable. The web can, for instance, bring classical music, art exhibitions, or the chance to learn a foreign language, to people who may otherwise miss out on these things. It can be a good source of entertainment and of accurate, useful, information.

But there is also a lot of poor quality material on the Internet – such as games that don't develop any useful skills, and unpleasant material with graphic violence or gross sexual content. People worry that some of these things encourage violence and crime in the real world, and may cause us psychological damage.

'I am determined not to… ingest foods or other items that contain toxins, such as certain TV programmes, magazines, books, films and conversations. I am aware that to damage my body or my consciousness with these poisons is to betray my ancestors, my parents, my society, and future generations.'

FIFTH BUDDHIST PRECEPT, THICH NHAT HANH

Ask yourself

◆ Do you think it is bad for people to spend too much time using the Internet for leisure rather than taking part in activities that involve other people?
◆ Is playing online games and other 'time-wasting' activities morally bad?
◆ Do violent games encourage real-life violence? Or could violent games provide a harmless way for people to release their aggression?

That's rubbish!

Junk email

Email addresses are sold to businesses that want to make money by selling things. If you give your email address to a website – to sign up for a game, perhaps – you may find that you get lots of junk email (called spam). This will usually offer you things that cost money. It might be more games – or it could be potentially damaging things, such as diet pills or pay-to-view adult websites.

Even where the offer is harmless, many people have to pay for the time emails take to download – and they may resent paying for emails that they're not interested in anyway.

Ask yourself

◆ What could we do about inappropriate junk email being sent to children?
◆ Should companies be entitled to send you advertising if they've paid for your email address?
◆ Should people be allowed to sell your details to other companies?

A corrupting influence?

Earlier in the book, we talked about countries that limit Internet access for political and religious reasons. Places like this may also ban websites in the hope of preserving national culture and tradition. People in some countries think that the ready availability of Western culture – especially from the USA – has led to the decline of other ways of life. Some people in developing countries may neglect local traditions in favour of aspects of Western

Western culture may seem attractive to people in the developing world. Is it right to keep it from them?

Traditional activities, such as this Indonesian shadow play, could be threatened by the spread of Western culture on the web. Should we try to preserve them?

culture that they see on television and the web. This could be anything from cartoons to pop music or online games. If people decide they want goods that aren't available to them, they may become resentful. The spread of Western culture may also cause rich local customs to die out.

Ask yourself

◆ Whose responsibility is it to protect traditional cultures and customs?
◆ How could this be done?
◆ Could access to Western culture on the Internet benefit other countries, as much as it causes them damage? If so, how?

Case study

The arrival of television in Fiji seems to be linked to a rise in eating disorders in Fijian girls. Traditionally, girls in Fiji are larger and eat more than girls in the West. When TV first came to Fiji in 1995, the recorded incidence of girls with eating disorders was 3 percent – but by 1998 it had risen to 15 percent. Girls with a TV were three times more vulnerable than other girls. This seems to be a result of seeing Western images of beauty – the West values a slim body shape. Television appears to be damaging people in Fiji – will the Internet do the same?

Who cares?

Who's looking after your safety as an individual user of the Internet? There's no global control, so it falls to local law makers and businesses to protect us. What measures should they take to help us avoid seeing upsetting materials?

Ratings systems

It's not realistic to expect any one company to monitor and rate every site that's put on the web, because this would require a vast amount of time and money. Government funding could help – but so far this is lacking.

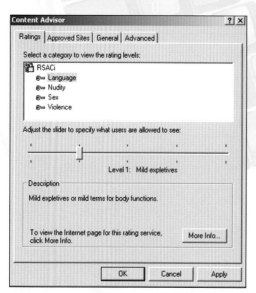

This rating system lets you pick what type of content you want to see on the web. But few people bother to use software like this – they may not even know they can.

As a starting point, a few independent bodies are setting up rating systems for websites that will give some indication of the content.

The Internet Content Rating Association is one of the largest. It doesn't rate websites itself, but offers the publishers of websites the chance to rate themselves. Their belief is that the publishers of adult sites don't generally want to upset children and will rate their sites as only suitable for over 18s, if that's appropriate.

This system is voluntary and relies on trust. Publishers of websites have to co-operate to rate their site, and users have to choose whether or not to use filtering software to block unrated sites. There is no law that enforces either publishers of websites or Internet users to control what's available or viewed.

Ask yourself

◆ Is it right that the law enforces a rating system on films, for example, but not on websites?
◆ Do we have a right to be warned if something is unpleasant or frightening?
◆ Do you think any rating system should be the responsibility of governments, of the Internet Service Providers, of the companies that make web browsers – or of someone else?

Should it be up to parents to monitor what their children see on the web, or should laws prevent the need for this?

Law and freedom

Where laws in some countries restrict what people can see on the web, in others there is no control of this kind. The USA values freedom of speech and freedom of information very highly and makes almost anything available online.

'Congress shall make no law... abridging the freedom of speech, or of the press.'

FIRST AMENDMENT,
US CONSTITUTION

In 1997, a new law called the Communications Decency Act was drawn up, aiming to restrict pornography and other unpleasant material. But it was ruled illegal by the US Supreme Court because it would restrict what could be published on websites and therefore limit freedom of information.

Ask yourself

◆ Do you agree with the freedom of information argument? Should people be able to publish and look at any material at all on the web, no matter how harmful it may be to others?
◆ Does society have a duty to protect people from unpleasant material on the web, in the same way that it aims to limit crime and abuse in the real world?

Who cares?

Limits of the law

Because the Internet crosses national boundaries, it is almost impossible to control. A country that wants to limit what its people can see and do online needs to filter all Internet traffic that goes in and out of the country. As we've seen, some places already do this – but it's hard to imagine it happening on a worldwide scale.

Even if we had strict international laws about what can be published on the web, there would always be some people who found ways round them. A banned website could still be hosted in a country that hadn't signed up to an agreement, or that didn't care about whether the law was enforced. And once a site is up on the web, it's there for all to see.

Knowing the risks

Children and other impressionable people are exposed to many risks if they use the Internet in an unprotected environment. They may be lured into chat and perhaps meetings with people who seem friendly but in fact intend harm – it's easy to be anonymous on the Internet, or to pretend to be someone you're not. People may see materials that upset them or even cause psychological damage. They might receive unpleasant spam email, be drawn into online gambling they can't afford, or be

Ask yourself

◆ Do you believe we need international laws relating to the Internet, covering what can be put on the web, the privacy of communications and other issues we have looked at in this book? If so, who should draw up these laws?

attracted by racist groups or harmful religious cults. In recent cases of child abductions and murders, police have investigated the children's computers to see if they have been used for chat, instant messaging, or other methods of contacting people who might have been dangerous. Not all parents know enough about the risks or the technology to make sure their children use only moderated chat rooms, visit suitable websites and keep their email addresses safe from unwanted mailings.

Case study

In June 2000, a convicted killer was arrested when he tried to meet up with and abduct a 14-year-old girl he had been chatting to over the Internet. The police were tipped off by a woman the girl had also chatted to online. The girl had told the woman about her planned meeting with the man.

Bill Gates is head of Microsoft, which produces the most popular web browser, Internet Explorer. Should browsers be developed so that you can't see unpleasant content unless you specifically change the settings?

Ask yourself

◆ Who should be responsible for protecting children and other people from harmful use of chat rooms and Internet messaging services?

Taking responsibility

Because of the way the Internet works, it's very difficult to make anyone responsible for what happens there. At the moment, anyone who feels they've been damaged by what they've seen or done online is on their own – it's down to individuals to avoid looking at harmful material. But many Internet users know little about the dangers, or how to avoid them, so is this fair? Perhaps we should expect the people who make money out of selling us computers, software and Internet connections to do more to protect people. Or is it more realistic to accept that we should all learn to take responsibility for our own wellbeing online?

Your own opinion

By now you should have enough background knowledge to start to form your own views on Internet technologies. These may be the same as or different from your friends'. But keep asking questions and finding things out. Try to understand all sides of the story. The more you learn, the stronger your arguments will be.

Further work

You can use the ideas on this page to help extend your interest in the Internet and related technologies.

Computer commandments

The following 'Ten Commandments', put together by the Computer Ethics Institute, suggest how people might use computers in a responsible way.

1 Thou shalt not use a computer to harm other people.

2 Thou shalt not interfere with other people's computer work.

3 Thou shalt not snoop around in other people's files.

4 Thou shalt not use a computer to steal.

5 Thou shalt not use a computer to bear false witness.

6 Thou shalt not use or copy software for which you have not paid.

7 Thou shalt not use other people's computer resources without authorization.

8 Thou shalt not appropriate other people's intellectual output.

9 Thou shalt think about the social consequences of the program you write.

10 Thou shalt use a computer in ways that show consideration and respect.

© Copyright 1998, Arlene Rinaldi and Florida Atlantic University

Write your own rules

Put together your own set of rules or guidelines for computer use – either for yourself or for your school. Can you also think of aspects of computer use that you feel should be covered by laws? Do you think laws should be national, international, or a combination of both?

Useful websites

www.icra.org
Website of the Internet Content Rating Association – explains ratings and has filters you can download.
http://worldkids.net/school/safety/Internet
Online safety tips and details of 'netiquette' – how to behave online.

Practise protection

Find out how well you are protected when you use the Internet at home, at school and anywhere else you go online – perhaps at the library or cybercafé. Ask about filtering software and other precautions that are in place. Do you think more could be done? Why not suggest ways in which improvements could be made? Think about ideas for teaching people to use computers safely and responsibly.

Glossary

censorship Restriction of information in order to stop people seeing or hearing anything that is considered unsuitable, unpleasant or damaging.

copyright A law that protects authors, artists and other creators by restricting how people can use creative work without paying for it.

download To copy information from a computer on the Internet onto your own computer.

encryption Putting a message into code so that it can't be understood without using the key to the code.

History folder A folder on your computer that keeps a list of the websites you have visited.

host (website) The computer that hosts a website is the one on which the files are stored and from which they are made available online.

human rights The basic rights people have to food, water, freedom and shelter.

intellectual property rights The rights people have to ownership of their ideas and artistic creations.

Internet traffic The movement of files over the Internet.

modem A device that connects a computer to the phone or cable network. It converts signals going to and from the computer so that they can be carried on the communications network and received on the computer.

moderated (chat room) Watched by someone who will interrupt or prevent unsuitable communication.

one-click buying Shopping on a website without giving your credit card details every time. The site stores your details and reuses them whenever you buy something.

online Connected to the Internet.

pirate copy An illegally made copy of a computer game, film or piece of music.

pornography Material with extreme sexual content.

surveillance Watching or spying on someone.

systems administrator The person who manages a computer network or system.

trapdoor A hidden part of a computer program that makes a computer accessible to others over the Internet. It is usually planted unknown to the computer's owner or user and is used to extract information secretly.

virus A program designed to disrupt data and to spread from computer to computer.

webcast Broadcast over the web of an event, such as a concert or debate.

Index